CW01159556

STRANGER IN THE MASK OF A DEER

Richard Skelton is a British artist. His work focuses on landscape and other-than-human studies. Between 2005 and 2011 he ran Sustain-Release, a private press music label dedicated to publishing his own landscape-oriented recordings. Since 2009 he has been co-director of the multi-media publishing house Corbel Stone Press, with the Canadian poet Autumn Richardson. Together they curate the biannual journal of eco-poetics and esoteric literature, *Reliquiae*. He is also founding member of the Notional Research Group for Cultural Artefacts and director of the Centre for Alterity Studies.

richardskelton.net

ALSO BY RICHARD SKELTON

Landings (2009)
Moor Glisk (2012)
Limnology (2012)
Beyond the Fell Wall (2015)
The Pale Ladder (2016)
The Look Away (2018)
Dark Hollow Dark (2019)
And Then Gone (2020)

Stranger in the Mask of a Deer

Richard Skelton

Penned in the Margins
LONDON

PUBLISHED BY PENNED IN THE MARGINS
Toynbee Studios, 28 Commercial Street, London E1 6AB
www.pennedinthemargins.co.uk

All rights reserved
© Richard Skelton 2021

The right of Richard Skelton to be identified as the author of this work has been asserted by him in accordance with Section 77 of the Copyright, Designs and Patent Act 1988.

This book is in copyright. Subject to statutory exception and to provisions of relevant collective licensing agreements, no reproduction of any part may take place without the written permission of Penned in the Margins.

First published 2021

Printed in the United Kingdom by TJ Books Limited

ISBN
978-1-908058-84-3

This book is sold subject to the condition that it shall not, by way of trade or otherwise, be lent, re-sold, hired out, or otherwise circulated without the publisher's prior consent in any form of binding or cover other than that in which it is published and without a similar condition including this condition being imposed on the subsequent purchaser.

CONTENTS

foreword 11

begin 15

dark 21

cast 25

dream 35

wake 55

it 65

before 71

sorrow 77

stranger 83

land 91

teacher 99

cave 103

story 111

flight 117

hunt 123

echo 135

mark 143

again 149

afterword 155

NOTES 159

ACKNOWLEDGEMENTS 165

for my mother
for my father

Stranger in the Mask of a Deer

FOREWORD

that this line appears new & complete & full formed & clear & perfectly distinct is an illusion a lie a betrayal a trick of the light that it has been cast down & broken & gathered & mended is nearer the truth that it is an arbitrary juncture in the process of endless reassembly is as good a definition as any as good bad indifferent as any

BEGIN

where do i begin
    father
    grandfather
    ancestor

begin here
    four & a half decades ago
    the bones cast
    a name given
    yours

this body
    this clot of muscles & blood
    skin & nerves

    but surely there were other forms
    other faces of the dice

how far can you cast your mind back
    as far as that hill ridge
    or the next

    begin with cold
    a burning cold

tell me where the cold lives

north of here
    the far back of hills
    nival rivers
    cryotic soils

& what is it
    this cold

it comes & it goes
    a huge white animal
    an unceasing hunger
    a quenchless thirst

but surely there are other forms
    other faces

whatever form it takes
    it is always the same
    do not cast yourself in its way
    it will take you to your death

& to my beginning

that also

DARK

    & when i look around i see darkness
        a great darkness reaching beyond sight

        & in that darkness other voices
        heard & not heard

                                come to me little one
                                      are you cold
                        i will wrap you in these skins
                                            come

    & when i look down i see my fathers hands
        & he his fathers hands
        & so on & so on
        down the long human chain

        father
        grandfather
        ancestor

do not follow
    whatever form it takes

                                      come to me little one

help me
    i cannot hold on
    i am falling

                                            come to me

& when i look down
    this clot
        of words letters glyphs

                        this

CAST

to cast the mind back
    six hundred generations
    bones muscles blood
    terminal pleistocene

ice veins
    debris tails
    boulder lobes

little one
    dreamer
    can you cast your mind back
    to before you were
    islanded

    do you remember it
    your death
    & rebirth

    your skin burning

    & the form of a great bear
    ursus arctos ursa major
    its thirst screams echoing the hills

mother
    grandmother
    ancestor

                                      come to me little one

i am cold

                you have slept these long years these long long years

burning

what did you dream of
    all those millennia under the ice

i dreamed a woman
    a woman singing
    gently singing cradle songs
    & carrying a sliver of ice

    a blade so sharp it could cleave the world

    but she bathed me cleaned me
    wrapped me in these skins
    & i slept

    i have slept these long years

    am i awake
    am i dreaming

& what did you see
    what did you see as you looked into her eyes

i cannot tell
    all i remember
    is that voice
    that melody

& all the while the stars overhead
    wheeling turning
    about the pole or post
    that holds the sky aloft

    & such a long time
    that even the fixed star itself
    ceded to another
    & so on & so on

    other forms always the same

each moving around
the great precessional gyre
waiting its turn
some twenty six millennia
to ascend
again

eight stars
eight ages
eight true directions

α umi	alpha ursae minoris or polaris
α cygni	alpha cygni or deneb
γ cep	gamma cephei or errai
α cep	alpha cephei or alderamin
α cygni	alpha cygni or deneb
δ cyg	delta cygni
α lyr	alpha lyrae or vega
τ her	tau herculis
α dra	alpha draconis or thuban

again & again & again

little bear
    dear one
    did you lick your paws in the stadial night
    curled in your hibernal nest deep beneath the ice
    as polaris gave way to errai to alderamin to deneb
    each shining bright & true above you
    watching over your sleep

i cannot tell

little bear
    dear one
    did you feel their lights rain down upon you
    in the long cold winter
    did deneb the luminous one
    awaken you with its bluewhite radiance

    & did you not feel it
    a great blade about your neck

am i awake
    am i dreaming

        she has left
                me
            dreaming

her thirst screams
    echoing the hills

& who is this
    who is it that comes from the south
    to wash in my nival rivers
    the blood from their hands

DREAM

how do i begin
   mother
   grandmother
   ancestor

   teach me how to see

begin with dream
   with what comes to you in the dark

nothing
   but this clot of images sounds senses

   but was there language there
   something spoken did i hear it right

   wake up
   it seemed to say with words made of silence
   wake up
   & the night & the day will bleed

am
i
awake

                    a blade so sharp it could cleave the world

                                                  am
                                                  i
                                            dreaming

last winter whilst on medication for chronic pain i began to have
visions in the darkness at the edge of sleep
a kind of phosphorescence hovering in the room above me
faint at first but unfurling growing in detail
alive

effects on the brain & central nervous system

tiredness headache weakness confusion disturbed
concentration disorientation delusions hallucinations elevated
mood & hyperactivity excitement anxiety restlessness
drowsiness dream & sleep disturbances numbness pins &
needles loss of coordination uncontrolled shaking abnormal
muscle movements slurred speech coma & fits

& the more i looked the more real they became
stark visions of limbs faces eyes impossible anatomies
suspended for minutes at a time in the silent darkness

& at first i was scared heart racing chest aching but as the
dark of winter deepened i began to accept them & welcome
them
like family

    delusions

                        hallucinations

                                                  family

    dream & sleep disturbances

                                                  family

what did you dream of
  all those millennia
  under the ice

all the men of my family gathered at the edge of the sea waiting
    & i am standing behind the others higher up & set apart
    & i see them four of them great bodies risen from the lowest
    stratum of ocean & my father with the great scar at his back
    stepping forward into the waters & the nearest of the four
    rising & wrapping its many arms around him taking him into
    its embrace

& all the while deneb raining down its bluewhite light upon us
& all the men of my family
at the edge of sleep
putting down their masks
their arms around each other

& no roads no paths to follow no pilgrimage routes no drove
    ways tracks or passes nothing but the scour of retreating
    ice nothing but gougemarks new riverbeds the edges of
    floodwaters moraines screes eskers drumlins

    & the ancestral world forgotten even unto itself & the new &
    alien & unknown

    & planes of rupture uncontrolled shaking the slow
    restlessness of soil the slurred speech of moss lichen artemisia
    & eventually scrub willow birch even pine
    eventually the green fullness of life

& a figure in those trees wearing strange skins glimpsed through
   the branches
   looking looking

this clot of skin & nerves
   rhizomes hyphae

& high in those branches the nests of birds long fledged long
   vanished
   & were they ever here i ask
   looking at the empty sky
   is it even possible i ask
   that thing called flight

wheeling turning

& moving through those trees the shapes of deer
   the shapes of deer & the curve of the earth & the light low shimmering dusk
   & they scatter the deer but one holds its ground looks at me stares me down
   & it is a deer & not a deer something other we both know it but i can say no more
   & i am already running
   running down the light low shimmering dusk

   why am i always running
   always running
   even in dream
   am i not yet ready
   am i still afraid

   mother i am still afraid

but it comes again
from a low bank of hills its pelt greywhite mottled with
darker colour shifting as if in mist
& its mask luminous impenetrable

but too quickly it is gone & i am left in unknowing

& yet for that moment when we held each others gaze
yes in that dark unfathomable instant
we both shared the same plume of blood

am i awake
    am i   bleeding

& of all those people
    five hundred generations ago
    who answered the call of the retreating ice
    north
    to a land beyond the limits of the known
    why have so few been found

what untold lineages are there in the karst
in the suffocating embrace of peat
in caves as yet undiscovered

what did they think

could they have held a land in the memory during those
thousands of years of absence when it was lost to ice

the passing of water from hand to hand
down the long human chain

it is unthinkable surely

five hundred generations

but was there language there
    something spoken
    did i hear it right

remember this it said
    there is nothing primeval nothing primordial nothing original
    nothing first there is only now it said the circuitry of life ever
    repeating & the you of then is just like the you of now & the
    you of then is looking front & back side to side up & down
    & just like you with a fist of narrow answers

to look back at a past that itself looks back
    to look back at the past that looks back at the past that looks
    back

& the circuitry of life ever repeating

& their faces are turned away & they are looking towards the
    horizon & to the hills & out to sea

    & how to face the horizon when the horizon is everywhere &
    all directions

& all directions simultaneous

& how to know their faces when i see them & when i see them they are wearing masks

& the look of me looking at you & the look of you looking at me to & fro to & fro
endless endless

& what if the figure i saw in the trees wearing strange skins
   glimpsed through the branches what if it was you all along looking for me across the great gulf of time

& the horror that is our knowledge of what has already passed & what has already passed an unendurable suffering
   & the horror that is our knowledge of what is to come & what is to come an insurmountable trial

& when i look down i see my fathers hands & he his fathers
hands & so on & so on down the long human chain

help me
    i   cannot

& in the fading dusk something made me look made me
look back up the darkening road & on the horizon an eye
opening a great scar in the gathering clouds & as i stood it
turned the colour of fire & the moon emerged & rose waxing
gibbous only a day from full & my eyes straining & my heart
straining to hold that luminous mask aloft & when it was
fully clear of the earth it seemed to fall then rise falling rising
pulsing rapidly & this flickering this squirming this atomic
dance seemed to speak to be a form of language

let go it said
we are both made of fire

bones muscles blood
   & the ice so cold it burned

but what did they think
   unthink think
   unthink

heart racing chest aching

& there in the dark beyond dark
   it comes it comes again

   an eye opening closing
   a form of language
   flickering

think of an other way it said
    think of this for example
    of the possibility of sacredness in all things
    the shimmer of life itself it said
    the firedance of atoms

burning flickering

& if you follow this way remember this it said
    that animal has its own life & plant has its own life & stone
    has its own life & hill has its own life & cloud has its own life
    & river has its own life & path has its own life & star has its
    own life & above has its own life & below has its own life

    & these lives are nothing if not inextricable
    & these lives are nothing if not inseparable
    & in that very affinity these lives are nothing less than equal
    & in that very affinity these lives are nothing more than equal
    & these lives are aspects of each other therefore
    & these lives are part of the same whole therefore

& life is nothing less & nothing more than singular therefore
& life is everywhere therefore
& nowhere is there that is not life therefore
& the world alive & thinking & feeling
& the world is consciousness experiencing itself endlessly &
as if for the first time
& the world is the self reflecting self
the self reflecting
self

eyes straining heart straining

& in this way words too are their own selves it said
    known unto themselves & hermetic
    & alive not lying on the page & dead on the mortuary slab
    for you to make your incision
    & in each encounter they sing resonant echoing in your skull
    long after their reading & were singing long before you came
    & will sing long after you leave
    if only you would listen & hear your own self sung into being

yes i said
    alive
    i have heard their lulling drone
    felt them gather me like pollen

but who have you been running from it said
    what has been hunting you all the long years of your life

i cannot remember

you do not want to know it said
    you do not want to know
    what you have forgotten

yes i said
    yes   yes

then follow it said

    & so we climb up through the roots of the hill & up its winding
stairs & at times so steep we are upside down but gravity has
no power here at the innards of the earth
    & there are days when the only sounds are the footsteps of
my guide & always ahead of me & out of sight
    & then the stairs vanish & all of a sudden & we are at a
narrow chamber in the roof of the hill & so very high & it
is sloping steeply down to a large fissure through which the
wind is blowing
    & i edge towards it no turning back nothing to be done &
the ground like grease & i look down through that chasm
in the rock & i see we are at the apex of a vast dome & the
earth within the hill a sickening distance & rivers & lakes &
marshes below so small so far away

    & climb down inside it says
        climb down inside
        this is how we fly

    & i woke to find my body strange unto myself
        the limbs not quite fitting together as they had before the
        joints extendable beyond their usual range & now i could
        fold my hand into the smallest point & fit my carcass into the
        narrowest crevice & something in my face had changed the
        eyes perhaps more sunken back into the skull the teeth more
        jutting & across my shoulders a great scar the skin charcoal
        black & i was burning & have never stopped burning

        & no images no sensations in the memory but something
        carried in the cells the knowledge of great violence yes my
        own utter destruction
        a disarticulation & rearticulation
        & a blade so sharp it could cleave the world

        & i saw myself & was myself & i saw myself & was myself &
        i saw myself & was myself & i saw myself & was myself

WAKE

tiredness headache weakness confusion

in the early not quite morning
    before the light bleaches all memory
    i go again looking for them
    those warm bodies of the unconscious

    but the cave mouth is deserted
    the hearth already cold
    & a wind is moving wildly through what they have left
    a scavenger like me

    i cannot hope to truly know them then
    cannot see their faces hear their language
    but perhaps i can infer something of their lives
    reconstructed in this scatter of discarded stone
    yes find in the shape of absence
    the thing itself

other forms other faces

they are not lost to me entirely then
    & as i leave the cave the wind cuts its melody from the fluted rocks
    there are other shatter marks more elusive than flint it seems to say
    & there scratched in ochre & low to the ground i see a figure wearing the mask of a deer
    looking back at me
    with blazing eyes

cast your mind back

                                the self reflecting self

& as day slowly dawns at my window a visitant circling rousing its feathers
a plume of language if only i knew it
& i kneel close a foot or less between us between my slack body & this taut wildness this wildness like a torrent

& it circles closer & i am afraid i am not afraid & i gently raise my hand & flatten it palm outwards on the glass
& it moves away at first
flight instinct
genetic memory

but then it circles back comes close starts to pick gently at the seams between my fingers
unpicking reality
& a deep wave of sadness overwhelms me
& a deep wave of hope

am i awake

                                                              uncontrolled shaking

am i dreaming

                                                       abnormal muscle movements

why have you come visitant
what is it that you must say

you have slept these long years these long long years

anxiety

                                                                    restlessness

    & i walk far & without direction
        as if to shake off a sleep that has lasted much too long

    at some point i notice a small brown bird
    it seems to wait until i draw near & then flies a little further
    again & again a circuit of meaning
    & the message i infer parcelled in this knot of form &
    movement is
    follow
    but am i wrong to look for signs symbols portents in the
    flights of birds the postures of animals
    do i not deny them their selfhood their autonomy

    & yet in the end is not my satellite self drawn by their very
    gravity
    their bright & burning spheres
    & i can do nothing but
    follow

do not follow
    whatever form it takes

later
    at some point between night & day i walk again
    sirius is ascending in the south east
    bright ascending
    a humped line through betelgeuse to capella
    crooked line

    the great bear ursa major rising to the north
    bright rising
    & vega the luminous one the beautiful one is bright
    through the haze to the north west
    bright through

    the world has discarded its mask of light
    its day disguise

    i have put down my mask i am alone unburdened
    i see more fully the world thicker fuller more ripe in its true
    dark form
    this aching realm of darkness is alive in its silence alive in its
    sounds
    alive

a fox barks from across the fields
calls to me from across the fields of mist
i too have put down my mask

i want to answer that call
to answer it in this my true form
but i am afraid
this my truth
afraid

later the return of day & a spasm of blue to the north east
pale blue

through the mist the earth & its true station is revealed
we are moving towards an abyss of light
a pale emptiness the ground underfoot a promontory leading
into that pale light
a nothingness
pale

the fox calls to me from the failing black
the fading black

says there is a way to reside within this ache of darkness
below the earth
calls me
a way
but i have put on my mask
away

why am i always turning away
why am i still afraid

numbness

                                                            disorientation

IT

& no turning back nothing to be done

can you not feel it it said
    pointing to the sky
    can you not feel it moving through you

    it is spilling within you
    pushing against your blood

    & you are human & you are animal & you are plant & you are stone & you are hill & you are cloud & you are river & you are path & you are star & you are above & you are below

    & the boundedness of your body is a lie
    your bounded mind a lie
    your identity a lie

    & let us not make distinctions when we talk of identity
    when we talk of itness
    when we talk of it

    & when you use the sacred word it
    let it mean the shimmer of life in all things
    animate or inanimate
    beyond the meagre confines of masculinity or femininity
    of him her he she

& your i as you see it is but a part of it
& any other term is but a division of it
is but an anagram of it
a reassembly
a reflection
an echo
of it

yes i said
    yes   yes

& remember this it said
    the boundlessness of the world means that you are never
    alone
    there are always presences
    always inherences
    things beyond sight

& each of your actions or inactions is storied in the world
& your being is the assembly of your doing & not doing &
your thinking & not thinking & nothing more than this

your life a series of encounters with the visible & invisible

& on the road before sunrise i found a hare newly dead but not
quite gone its corpse still warm its blood pooled around a
great scar at its back

& though dead it seemed to be holding on
but for what i could not say

& there in the trees nearby i sensed a figure
a figure sensed through the branches
looking looking

& i picked up the body & i laid it in the heather
thinking of the long low embrace of soil
the many hands of grasses

& as i stood there i felt its lifehood fade

& when i looked up the figure was gone
away through the branches & not looking back
& the sun just coming up
just passing over the horizon

BEFORE

& what was there before the flood i said
ice it said

& before the archipelago i said
the dogger umbilicus it said

& before the wildwood
the plain & the age of grasses

& before albion
europa

& what was there before metallurgy i said
the science of flint it said

& before patriarchy i said
union it said

& before husbandry
reciprocity & the hunt

& before standing stones
the axis mundi

& before chambered tombs
the hollows within the earth

& what was there before father sun i said
the fixed star & its bluewhite radiance it said

& before mother earth i said
the slow restlessness of soil it said

& before polytheism
the plant & animal & mineral other

& before monotheism
the gaze of a deer

& before god & the devil
nival rivers

& what was there before worship i said
respect it said

& before reverence i said
respect it said

& before sacrifice
respect

SORROW

& life is everywhere & nowhere is there that is not life

but how to make my way through the world i said
    when each step impinges upon an other
    when each action displaces or absorbs an other
    when everything must eat & be eaten

    & how to hold that knowledge in the mind & not be
    paralysed by horror fear anxiety

    did i take from you unnecessarily
    did i not give of myself when it was my time

yes it said
    horror but also joy
    horror & joy commingled
    everything commingling
    endlessly dissolving & resolving
    moving to & fro to & fro
    everything contingent on one another
    touching one another
    piercing one another

i cannot hold on

let go it said
    & you will see that you are held

i cannot
    i am afraid
    i am still afraid

& so turn away it said
    & forget & find solace in that forgetting

    & rather than bleed afresh each day grow that skin which you think contains you separates you identifies you

    & that very forgetting will allow you to move through the world without feeling

but i do not want this i said
    i do not want this numbness

then consider this it said
    there are ways other than forgetting
    & the simplest of these is sorrow

    & in its expression you are returned to the world
    & the world is returned to you

    & the corollary of this sorrow is gratitude

this is a world of sorrow i said

yes it said
    yes   yes

STRANGER

am i still who i think i am
    you who know me would say so
    but you have not seen what i have seen
    & so i must seek out an other

    & i walk far & without direction
    as if to shake off a fear that has lasted much too long

    & there ahead of me a figure
    a figure on all fours standing waiting

    stranger
    may i come to you
    as i am wearing a kindred skin
    a skin given to me by my mother
    & the one who gave it to her
    is returned to the soil
    is returned to the waters
    as i will return to the soil
    as i will return to the waters
    & i wear it in deference & in sorrow
    & i wear it like life

so that i might come to you
so that you might come to me

stranger
show your face to me your true face
show yourself as i show myself
look i have put down my mask

& i will put down these points if you put down those points
the time is not right for killing

show yourself therefore stranger
as i you so you me
& we shall be known to each other

& you put down your points
& you put down your mask
& we stand together prone

& at first i am scared heart racing chest aching

& the look of me looking at you
& the look of you looking at me
to & fro to & fro

& who do you see when you look at me
& what do you see when you look at me

we are alike you & i it says
   we are alike

   & you feel it just as i do
   in the spaces between your joints

   hunted

yes

    this slack body
    & a river moving through me
    its edges beyond reach
    always beyond reach

you have opened your body & you have opened your self so that
    others may be spared
    but you will suffer because of this

    you will suffer as we suffer

i am burning & have never stopped burning

this is a path of suffering
    & so now we are known you & i
    now we are known to each other

    joined by this suffering

    & so let us go our separate ways on this day
    on this day let us go

    but on another day
    one of us will die

& i am already running
    running down the light low shimmering dusk

LAND

& deneb gives way to delta cygni to vega

& those people who returned five hundred generations ago
   to this northborn peninsula
   how did they greet a land made new
   still writhing amniotic

   when life is the endless to & fro of knowing
   how did they make their way across an unknown terrain

   & what good would i be
   a man of four & a half decades
   a man with youth behind him
   with too much fear to carry & senses blunted by the years
   a weight to further slow their movement
   a useless burden to be shed

& no roads no paths to follow no pilgrimage routes no drove
   ways tracks or passes

nothing but the hoof prints of the animal other

& the living language of the soil

i am the deers tail
    i am the elks tail
    i am the reindeers tail
    i am the tarpans tail

other forms other faces
    always the same

& i follow them wherever they are headed
    & i follow them even until death

& the world alive & thinking & feeling

great northern plain
    as you have made their way
    so make mine

& not one but many
    each the same
    each different
    no self but in the other
    no other except the self

hill valley hollow
    as they must consume the blood & fat of your body
    so i must consume them

    & the fixed star above us the same & the great bear rising & falling & the river in the sky always flowing & the pleiades above us the same
    & when i am done i will return their bones to you so that you may in turn consume them & return them to the world complete & full formed through a hole of your making

muscles & blood
    skin & nerves

river pool bog
    i know you can make the tarpan fall
    can mire the deer & elk
    can drown the reindeer in its crossing

    but then you must wait for some scavenger or for time itself
    to divest the bones of their fleshy casings
    whereas i can return them to you before they are cold

    i am the bears tooth
    i am the felids tooth
    i am the hawks tooth
    i am the wolfs tooth
    as you have made their way
    so make mine

& so each movement north a conversation each step a
   negotiation an uncovering of ancestral ties long forgotten

yes it said
   speech gesture dream vision
   a giving & receiving
   a to & fro

   but remember this it said
   there is nothing primeval nothing primordial

   there was no great journey
   no cardinal encounter with the inchoate

   nothing but the slow restlessness of soil
   the slurred speech of moss lichen artemisia

   the north rewritten in greens & browns
   & storied by warm bodies
   a line at a time
   a life at a time

& a hundred thousand lives & a hundred thousand deaths
   & the screams of women as they birthed the human world
anew over & over

& their blood & the emmenagogue earth

& their birth screams echoing the hills
   & the fires doused

& who is this
   who is it that comes from the south
   to wash in my nival rivers
   the blood from their hands

TEACHER

& yet for that moment when we held each others gaze

    & those people
        five hundred generations ago
        who left the refuges of the south
        & followed the dwindling herds northwards

    was there an other among you

    was there one of your group who was not of your own
    one who walks on all fours & with teeth for a name

    & did such a one teach you to be with animals
    to be with yourselves

    & were you wilded by its company
    made new
    again & again
    by the look of it
    looking at you

the self reflecting
    self

CAVE

& how to know their faces when i see them
& when i see them they are wearing masks

how far can you cast your mind back

    to a cave south of here & the single shattered rib bone of an
    animal that did not return to the north when the ice retreated
    & to a figure scratched thereon
    a figure of vaguely human shape
    no more than five centimetres in height
    its penis erect & its face pointed

    its face pointed as if wearing a mask
    its face pointed like that of a bear

    & this the only carved figure of vaguely human shape found
    as yet on the entire peninsula
    found as yet in a form that can be held in the hand

    a bone carried northwards from the great steppes
    a bone scratched with a shape that is both human & not
    human
    a relic of a time before
    the journey north

a time before this time

to look back at a past that itself looks back
    to look back at the past that looks back at the past that looks back

    anthropomorph
    therianthrope
    dancing between the shape of one thing & the shape of another

    will you speak
    what is it that you must say

who do you see when you look at me
    what do you see when you look at me

dancer

yes

        yes

& yes will you speak
   will you say something
   of the past

   for instance
   which of your lines came first
   which cut which incision
   that on its own begged another & another
   until they made a face a body a figure a world
   a story of creation

   & how do those lines connect & pierce one another
   so that they make a face a body a figure a world
   a story of creation

& do they know of each other
accept each other
welcome each other

& do they know that they make a face a body a figure a world
& acknowledge thereby their place in a larger story

a story of creation
that is ongoing in each & every moment
endless endless

or is it simply enough to acknowledge
proximity & union

that our lines connect & pierce one another
in a great picture that we cannot see

& so these marks i leave here
legible now but for how long

& the words they make
are they my own

did i write them

for i have felt them gather me like pollen
or collect on my surfaces like dew
move through me like mist or wildfire

& so is something else speaking us
writing us
as it passes among us
are we landforms that have mistaken weather for thought
for selfhood

& these words endlessly assembled disassembled reassembled
& these bodies endlessly assembled disassembled reassembled

& the slow restlessness of soil

STORY

there is a one who was before us
    though not the first
    there is a one who was before us
    though not one of us

    it is the one whose sacred body was divided
    the one whose tears became the oceans
    the one whose bones became the mountains
    the one whose muscles became the soil
    the one whose skin became the tundra
    the one whose hairs became the grasses
    the one whose veins became the rivers
    the one whose hands became the creatures of the earth
    the one whose tail became the creatures of the sky
    the one whose feet became the creatures of the sea

    & the upright spear that pierces its skull
    & although not the first
    & who threw it no one knows
    that spear through its skull is the pole or post that holds the
    sky aloft that keeps the skys tent from falling
    though not the first & only just for now

& so sleep little one sleep
though you are dead & your body transformed beyond reckoning
a disarticulation & rearticulation

& so sleep little one sleep
so that we might live still

am i awake
    am i dreaming

               she has left
                          me
                    dreaming

& each year we will find a stranger to mark in your memory

    one who sleeps in the winter
    one abandoned by its mother

    & we will retell the story of your transformation on its body
    & give it the life after life after life after life

    & dismember & remember

    this clot of stories fables myths

                                this

FLIGHT

mother
    grandmother
    ancestor

    you who have travelled beyond the limits of the known
    you who have flown with the animal others
    among the stars above the earth
    among the stars below the earth

    help me

begin with dream
    with the world within the world
    with the world behind the world
    with the world beyond the world
    everything begins there

    will you come with me
    will you come with me
    i will find it & i will send it to you

but remember this
our human form is but a covering
is but a borrowing
our shapes are not our own

& we ride in her song so far so very far that the stars themselves
  begin to shift
  & deneb gives way to delta cygni to vega
  & we fly to the very fixed star itself & i see a star no more but
  the opening of a cave & a vast tundra laid out beyond & a
  great wind is blowing & a burning cold in the bones

wait here she says
wait here
& she is gone

& i lie in the mouth of the cave for what seems like millennia
& i lie in the mouth of the cave until the time is right

& it comes to me at last & it comes to me at last
& it is a woman & not a woman something other we both
know it but i can say no more
& her skin soft & warm beneath furs & the touch of it & the
touch of it
& she wraps her arms around me
taking me into her embrace
moving me to & fro
& i want to yield to her
& i want to yield

& at the last moment she puts down her mask

& all i see are antlers
& all i see are jutting teeth

& i hear these words in the air between us
i will be quickness itself my dear one
i will be quickness itself

& it is suddenly dark all around us
& i try to turn away in fear but i am held & i cannot move

& our eyes & our eyes & our eyes & our eyes

& i try to scream but i cannot
& i feel the edge of a blade
& i feel its point
piercing penetrating rupturing my skin

mother
grandmother
ancestor

when i return you are standing over me
singing shaking
the whole tent shaking
& when i look down i see blood in my hands

HUNT

what are the things that matter when movement is life &
   stillness is what comes after
   when those who carry nothing but their flesh are ahead of us
   & we who follow must pretend to the same condition
   when thought itself has weight & must be shed at the banks
   of every river
   these words i leave here to make way for their silence
   these words i leave here to read their marks in the soil

   help me
   mother
   grandmother
   ancestor

   you who have ascended the dark above the earth
   you who have descended the dark below the earth
   what do you see

i see it do you not see it
    it has hunted us in our dreams
    it has haunted us in our dreams
    & it has maimed us killed us time over time
    but it returned us to life & we were made new & stronger &
    when we awoke the gift of death not looked for & the gift of
    life not looked for
    was ours

help me
    father
    grandfather
    ancestor

    why must i show myself at the last
    why must i put down my mask

there are other ways other beliefs
    but ours is the way of knowing my dear one
    ours the way of knowing

& the mask may help you may bring you close
but in the last moment you must show yourself
you must show the other that you have met before
& then ask

even killing is a negotiation
each movement a conversation
a giving & receiving

& as the great northern plain is open
so must you be
this is our way

mother
    grandmother
    ancestor

    help me see
    is it the right time
    help me see
    is it the right time

look into its eyes & ask my little one
    & you will be told if it is the right time

father
    grandfather
    ancestor

    i will hunt it in the world beyond the world
    & you will hunt it in the world of flesh
    & together we will make it
    & together we will make it right

    & you burn the bones saved for this purpose
    for the task of augury for the premonitory act
    & you cast them on the ground & you read the marks
    appearing there & they point to the west & to the lowlands
    & you set off through the hills

& i must engorge myself & empty myself
& i must discover myself & discard myself
assemble disassemble assemble disassemble

& i am standing in the river the great river the dark river
& its edges are within me & its edges are beyond reach
& i can feel my stomach acid rising
& a sweat is covering my skin

& i put on the mask saved for this purpose
& the act of likening is upon me
& the act of likening is here

& i begin my song & i begin my song
& i sing & i sing & i sing & i sing

i am the land & the ice that formed it
i am the great bear & the little bear
i am the mother & the father

ask my dear little one just ask

i the human i the animal i the plant i the stone
    i the blade found at the heart of the flint
    i the fire of its transformation
    i the strike that shaped it made it
    i the shattered sound of its becoming
    i the sinew that bound it to the shaft

a blade so sharp it could cleave the world

i the slope that stands between us
    i the slope that hides us from each other
    i the slope that offers this vantage
    i the plain that joins us together
    i the plain that narrows our distance
    i the plain that renders this moment

    & i have tracked you for what seems like millennia
    & i have tracked you until the time is right
    & it comes to this & it comes to this

& this death i offer is not your ending
this death i offer is your beginning

& the circuitry of life ever repeating

& there ahead a thin copse of birch alder willow & the reeds & rushes of marshes behind & the ground underfoot so soft so wet so shifting

& moving through those trees the shapes of deer
the shapes of deer & the curve of the earth & the light low shimmering dusk

& they scatter the deer but one holds its ground looks at me stares me down
& it is a deer & not a deer something other we both know it but i can say no more

i see you
    it says with words made of silence
    i see you do you not see me

& i see it & i see it wears my skin & i see it wears my blood & its eyes are the eyes of my father & its eyes are the eyes of my mother & my hands are shaking & my legs are shaking & my mind is shaking

    & i put down my mask
    & i show myself
    & i hear these words in my mouth as if from a stranger
    i will be quickness itself my dear one
    i will be quickness itself

    & in the world of flesh i will return your bones to the waters
    & in the world of flesh i will return your bones to the soil
    so that you may come again & give yourself again
    trust me you know it is so
    so tell me
    is it the right time
    is it the right time

will you kill me it asks
    will you kill me
    will you kill yourself

& it turns to leave but my hand is raised in hunger & in desire
    & in fear & too late the shaft leaves my grip too late the
    blade finds its mark & i see a great scar at its back a bloody
    eye opening looking back at me looking back
    & it turns & bares its jutting teeth & screams
    & it stumbles into the waters its legs buckling shaking & the
    reeds & rushes wrapping their many arms around it
    taking it into their embrace

    & i fall to my knees & i fall & i fall i am fallen

    & our blood & our lives & our blood & our lives & our
    blood & our lives & our blood & our lives

the self reflecting
    self

& in the world of flesh
   in the world of echoes
   my father & the deer
   the deer & my father
   & their meeting inevitable
   this moment inevitable

   & no way to tell him
   no way to let him know
   that the time was not right
   that the time is not right

   & the deer looking back at him the deer looking back with
   vacant eyes & he slides the blade between its ribs
   & gives it the gift of death not looked for
   the gift of life

   & it screams & it screams & it screams & it screams

ECHO

& many petitions of sorrow made ever after
    & many reparations sought
    & many offerings made unto nival rivers
    & many rituals called into being
    & so on & so on
    the passing of blood from hand to hand
    down the long human chain

    & that scream echoing the far back of hills
    that scream echoing & not diminishing but resounding &
    resonating & amplifying down the years
    a curse sung across the great gulf of time

will you kill me it asked
    will you kill me
    will you kill yourself

& when i look back at those events in oneiric memory
    i watch the spear leave my hand & head towards the deer
    & the spear heading towards it heading towards it heading towards it heading towards it
    & the spear heading towards me heading towards me heading towards me heading towards me
    & i fall to my knees & i fall

planes of rupture

                                              uncontrolled shaking

erectus
    afarensis
    ancestor

    is the deers cry but an echo of our own
    a blood memory surfacing with each wound inflicted

for so many deaths have you received not looked for
so many sharp & narrow lives

but at what point in our lineage did we return transformed
when did the night & the day bleed together
from which wound did the killer in us emerge

& is this the true curse
this the darkness from which we cannot run
that we wear the mask of both the hunted & the hunter
that we have seen the life lived on both sides

each life the same
    each life different

i am the life that lives on life
    i am the destroyer
    but something carried in the cells the knowledge of great
    violence yes my own utter destruction
    i am the destroyed

& in that moment of death
is there surrender
is there acceptance
are we reconciled at the last

for i have suffered & give only that which was given to me

& there at the blade edge of life i see a figure
a figure skinned in ochre & wearing the mask of a deer
looking back at me
with blazing eyes

burning flickering

was there language there
    something spoken
      did i hear it right

remember this it said
    in the moment of your death
    the knowing will come to you at last

    the knowing that you have died innumerable times
    & given death innumerable times
    & returned innumerable times

    & the joy in knowing that there is no end
    & the horror in knowing that there is no end

& the circuitry of life ever repeating

& all the people you have known it said
    & all the people who have known you
    each human animal plant stone
    each hill cloud river word
    echoing commingling

this clot of life
    this clot of being

am i awake
    am i dreaming

& the vast immeasurable dark above the earth
    & the vast immeasurable dark below the earth

MARKS

these marks i leave here
    legible now but for how long

    & of all those people
    five hundred generations ago
    who answered the call of the retreating ice
    north
    to a land beyond the limits of the known
    why have so few been found

    what have they left us that we can interpret as language

    but we have exhumed their bones from the earth
    from the long low embrace of soil
    & we think that we have wisdom

    yet all i see is a darkness
    a darkness reaching beyond sight

    & there in the trees figures wearing strange skins glimpsed
    through the branches
    looking looking

& their knowing that we have died innumerable times
& given death innumerable times
& returned innumerable times

& the circuitry of life ever repeating

& they turn away from us
their forms
                        fading

help me
i cannot hold on
i am falling

hold on

& when i look down i see my fathers hands & he his fathers
hands & so on & so on down the long human chain

& our hands holding on to each other in that vast
immeasurable dark holding on to each other

& our hands holding on to each other
our hands holding on in that vast immeasurable dark
holding on

& that vast immeasurable dark holding on

AGAIN

& climb down inside
climb down inside

& we climbed through the air for what seemed like millennia & we climbed through the air until the time was right & then my guide took my hand & spoke to me & said

do you not hear them
listen they are coming

& inside the hill i remember it now yes inside the hill i remember

i heard the clicking of innumerable hooves & the sounds of a herd vast beyond telling & look my guide said to me look you must open your eyes & i opened my eyes & what i saw was a great gathering of people yes a herd of people who looked just like me but i did not know them yes just like me but strangers & they turned & looked & they turned & looked & some looked with eyes of joy & some looked with eyes of horror & some spoke with voices of kindness & some spoke with voices of anger & i felt their many hands upon me & i felt their many lives upon me

& from nowhere & all directions simultaneous a great wind began to blow & somewhere up above it all a voice a womans voice gently singing

    & i turned to my guide in fear
    & i turned to my guide & wept

    mother
    father
    ancestor

yes this is where you begin it said
    this where you begin
    again

    & yes
    what mask
    what covering
    will you wear the next time
    when you pass through here
    through the hole in the earth i have made for you

& how will you greet the world
how greet the world anew
when you are made new
still writhing amniotic

as polaris gives way to errai to alderamin to deneb

AFTERWORD

so many erasures so many deletions so many effacings so many extinctions so many wipings out so many annihilations so many occlusions so many obscurations so many coverings so many suffocations so many burials so many maskings so many eclipses so many blottings so many overwritings so many obfuscations so many shroudings so many secretings so many hidings so many suppressions so many cover ups so many hush jobs so many smoke screens so many hoaxes so many decoys so many con games so many scams

NOTES

Stranger in the Mask of a Deer is a call-and-response from the present to the past, going back to the end of the last glaciation, when the land that is now Britain emerged from beneath the retreating ice sheets. During this remote epoch of prehistory, the environment would have most resembled the arctic and sub-arctic tundra of today's Siberia and North America. It is thought that the peoples venturing north from continental Europe were hunter-gatherers, and perhaps certain tentative analogies can be drawn between their ways of life and the lives of those occupying the circumpolar north in the historical period. In its attempt to imagine aspects of that lost and distant Late Upper Palaeolithic European culture, this book therefore draws upon anthropological discussions of circumpolar hunter-gatherer societies, although it pursues a distinctly singular, highly personal trajectory and makes no claims to be representative. The people of the past were no more a homogenous group than are those of the present.

1 [*stranger*] The title owes a debt to that of John Haines's collected poems, *The Owl in the Mask of the Dreamer*.
27 [*six hundred generations*] The Quaternary period has been marked by repeated cycles of cold (stadial) and warm (interstadial). The most recent sustained cold period culminated in the Last Glacial Maximum, which in Britain and Ireland is thought to have occurred between approximately 27,000 and 21,000 years ago. During this phase, the crudescence of ice is thought to have forced humans and

other animals southwards across the Dogger land-bridge, and to glacial refuges on the greater European continent. In *Stranger in the Mask of a Deer* a generation is equated to 30 years. The poem therefore begins 18,000 years ago, as the ice began to slowly recede after the Last Glacial Maximum. See Richard C. Chiverrell & Geoffrey S. P. Thomas, 'Extent and timing of the Last Glacial Maximum (LGM) in Britain and Ireland: a review', *Journal Of Quaternary Science*, 25:4, 2010, pp. 535–549.

27 [*little one*] The land of Britain is mythologically conceived of as a little bear, in contradistinction to the great bear, its mother, or cold itself.

28 [*great bear*] The special regard that humans reserve for the ursine species is thought to have considerable time depth, dating back to at least 26,000 BP. See Mietje Germonpré and Riku Hämäläinen, 'Fossil Bear Bones in the Belgian Upper Paleolithic: The Possibility of a Proto Bear-Ceremonialism', *Arctic Anthropology*, Vol. 44, No. 2, 2007, pp. 1–30.

31 [*precessional gyre*] I.E. axial precession. The gradual shift in an astronomical body's rotational axis. For the earth, this cycle takes approximately 25,772 years. The terrestrial effect of this is the appearance of a cycle of different 'pole' stars.

32 [*deneb*] As Britain began to emerge from the Last Glacial Maximum, c. 18,000 BP, Deneb would have been the pole star.

40 [*all the men of my family*] Many of the dream elements in the poem were a consequence of taking an infusion of mugwort (*Artemisia vulgaris*). The Artemisia genus itself is attested in the Late-glacial pollen record for the north-west of England. See Winifred Pennington,

'Vegetation History In The North-West Of England: A Regional Synthesis', *Studies In The Vegetational History Of The British Isles*, Eds. D. Walker and R.G. West, 1970, pp. 46–51.

42 [*birds long fledged*] In Siberian tradition, some 'fledgling' shamans were metaphysically nurtured in nests high in the 'World Tree'. See Joan Halifax, *Shamanic Voices: A Survey of Visionary Narratives*, 1979, p. 17.

44 [*five hundred generations*] I.E. 15,000 years ago. Human bones found in Gough's Cave, Somerset, have been dated to 12,590 ±50 radiocarbon years BP (OxA-17849), which in real-world 'solar' years is: 15,176 – 14,603 BP (Using Oxcal 4.4. and the IntCal 20 Calibration Curve). See R.M. Jacobi & T.F.G. Higham, 'The early Lateglacial re-colonization of Britain: new radiocarbon evidence from Gough's Cave, southwest England', *Quaternary Science Reviews*, 28, 2009, pp. 1895–1913.

54 [*a disarticulation & rearticulation*] For the relevance of bodily dismemberment and reassembly to shamanic initiation, see Piers Vitebsky, 'Shamanism', *Indigenous Religions, A Companion*, Ed. Graham Harvey, 2000, p. 60. For its significance in the ritual deposition of animal remains, see Tim Ingold, 'Hunting, sacrifice and domestication', *The Appropriation of Nature*, 1986, pp. 246–7.

69 [*& though dead it seemed to be holding on*] The idea that an animal's sentience lingers after death, in order to observe how respectfully its remains are treated by humans, is a key concept in some Indigenous circumpolar worldviews. See, for example, Erica Hill, 'Animals as Agents: Hunting Ritual and Relational Ontologies in Prehistoric Alaska and Chukotka', *Cambridge Archaeological Journal*, 21:3, 2011, p. 409.

73 [*dogger umbilicus*] Doggerland, a low region that connected Britain to continental Europe. It was flooded c. 8,500 BP. For a chronological context, see Paul Preston, 'The Mesolithic Period', *The Handbook of British Archaeology*, Eds. Roy and Lesley Adkins, and Victoria Leitch, 2008, p. 24.

73 [*europa*] Referring to the greater European continent, rather than the Greek mythical figure.

74 [*the axis mundi*] The axis of the world. Here more strictly relating to the world pillar or pole, which in certain circumpolar worldviews is thought to hold up the sky and keep it from falling. See Åke Hultkrantz, 'A new look at the world pillar in Arctic and sub-Arctic religions', *Shamanism and Northern Ecology*, Ed. Juha Pentikäinen, 1996, pp. 31–50.

75 [*mother earth*] Here specifically referencing the concept of a maternal goddess important to later agricultural peoples as responsible for the bounty of the earth, rather than the primordial earth mother depicted in some creation myths as joined in sexual union with 'father heaven'. See E.J. Michael Witzel, *The Origins of the World's Mythologies*, 2012, pp. 128–131.

86 [*your true face*] The use of masks in the poem draws upon anthropological discussions of Indigenous ontologies, filtered and refracted by my own dream imagery. A key reference is the work of Alfred Irving Hallowell (1892–1974), who introduced the term 'other-than-human person' to describe how the Northern Ojibwa have a broader, more holistic conception of personhood that isn't limited solely to humanity. Hence, in *Stranger in the Mask of a Deer*, the mask in many instances symbolises a person's visible exterior. In encounters with

others, the *putting down* of masks is at once an act of self-revelation, and also a way of acknowledging inner likeness and shared personhood. See Alfred Irving Hallowell, 'Ojibwa Ontology, Behavior and World View', *Culture in History: Essays in Honor of Paul Radin*, Ed. Stanley Diamond, 1960.

94 [*tarpan*] An ancient and now-extinct subspecies of wild horse, *Equus ferus ferus*.

95 [*great northern plain*] An area combining the modern-day West Lancashire Coastal Plain and The Fylde.

101 [*walks on all fours*] 'Based on substantial archaeological and genetic evidence, a Late Upper Paleolithic (ca. 16,000 BP) timing for dog domestication is generally accepted.' Angela Perri, 'A wolf in dog's clothing: Initial dog domestication and Pleistocene wolf variation', *Journal of Archaeological Science* 68, 2016, pp. 1–4.

105 [*a cave south of here*] Pin Hole Cave, Derbyshire. In 1928 A.L. Armstrong discovered the carving of 'a masked human figure in the act of dancing a ceremonial dance' on a fragment of woolly rhinoceros rib bone (*Coelodonta antiquitatis*). See A. Leslie Armstrong, 'Pin Hole Cave Excavations, Creswell Crags, Derbyshire. Discovery Of An Engraved Drawing Of A Masked Human Figure.', *Proceedings of the Prehistoric Society of East Anglia*, Volume 6, Issue 1, 1929, pp. 27–29.

105 [*an animal that did not return*] According to Jacobi *et. al.*, the woolly rhinoceros became extinct in Britain after c. 35,000 BP. It seems most plausible to me that the item was brought to Creswell Crags as an already carved artefact, given that it would surely be unusual for a traveller to carry an unadorned bone hundreds of miles

north from the greater European continent. See Roger M. Jacobi, et. al., 'Revised radiocarbon ages on woolly rhinoceros (*Coelodonta antiquitatis*) from western central Scotland: significance for timing the extinction of woolly rhinoceros in Britain and the onset of the LGM in central Scotland', *Quaternary Science Reviews* 28, 2009, pp. 2551–2556.

113 [*the one whose sacred body was divided*] 'The carving up of the primordial giant may represent a very old stage of (Laurasian) mythology, going back to Stone Age hunter times.' E.J. Michael Witzel, *The Origins of the World's Mythologies*, 2012, p. 120. In this example, the giant is a bear.

127 [*ask*] For a discussion of real-world consensual killing, see Tim Ingold, 'Totemism, animism and the depiction of animals', *The Perception of the Environment*, 2011, p. 121.

133 [*it stumbles into the waters*] This encounter is partially modelled on the discovery of an ancient elk (*Alces alces*) at High Furlong, Poulton, Lancashire. The fossil assemblage included human-made barbed points, suggesting that the animal had been wounded before it died. The commonly accepted theory is that the elk had evaded capture only to drown in a pool. See Hallam, *et al.*, 'The Remains of a Late Glacial Elk Associated with Barbed Points from High Furlong, Near Blackpool, Lancashire', *Proceedings of the Prehistoric Society*, Volume 39, December 1973 , pp. 100–128.

ACKNOWLEDGEMENTS

This work was created with the financial support of a PhD Scholarship from Manchester Metropolitan University, 2017–2020.

Gratitude, as ever, to Autumn Richardson, for your inspiration and guidance.

Thanks to Dori Beeler, David Borthwick, Tom Chivers, Rosie Dunnett, Ben Edwards, Paul Evans, Tim Ingold, Jonathan Lageard, Jared Lindahl, Robert Macfarlane, Jean Sprackland, Christopher Thornhill and Kate Wilkinson.

Especial thanks to David Cooper.